ASIA

by Madeline Donaldson

Lerner Publications Company • Minneapolis

Lerner Publications Company
A division of Lerner Publishing Group, Inc.
241 First Avenue North
Minneapolis, MN 55401 U.S.A.

Website address: www.lernerbooks.com

Words in **bold type** are explained in a glossary on page 30.

Library of Congress Cataloging-in-Publication Data

Donaldson, Madeline.
    Asia / by Madeline Donaldson.
        p.   cm. — (Pull ahead books)
    ISBN-13: 978-0-8225-4721-1 (lib. bdg. : alk. paper)
    ISBN-10: 0-8225-4721-X (lib. bdg. : alk. paper)
    1. Asia—Geography—Juvenile literature. I. Title.
II. Series.
DS5.92.D66 2005
915–dc22   2004005331

Manufactured in the United States of America
7 – PP – 9/14/12

Photographs are used with the permission of: ©David Keaton/CORBIS, p. 3; © John Elk III, pp. 6, 15; © Betty Crowell, p. 7; ©Dean Conger/CORBIS, pp. 9, 10–11; © TRIP/M. Barlow, pp. 12–13; © Art Directors/TRIP, p. 14; ©Galen Rowell/CORBIS pp. 16–17; © Victor Englebert, p. 18; © A. A. M. Van der Heyden/Independent Picture Service, p. 19; © TRIP/A. Tovy, p. 20; © TRIP/T. Lester, p. 21; © Keren Su/CORBIS, pp. 22–23; © Bachmann/The Image Finders, p. 24; © Trip/A. Kuznetsov, p. 25; © Novastock/The Image Finders, pp. 26–27. Maps on pp. 4–5, 8, and 29 by Laura Westlund.

Where can you climb the world's tallest mountain?

The **continent** of Asia! A continent is a big piece of land.

Arctic Ocean

North America

Atlantic Ocean

Pacific Ocean

South America

Antarctica

There are seven continents on Earth.
Asia is the largest of all.

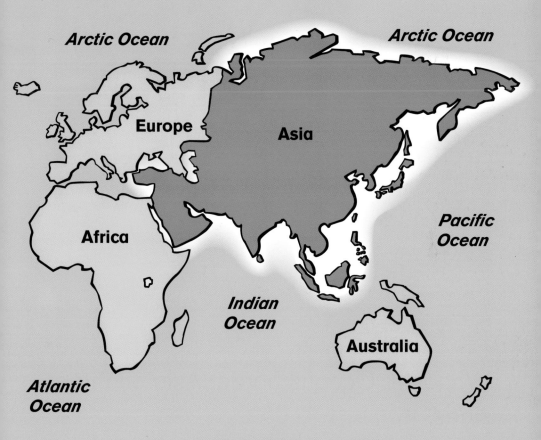

Arctic Ocean

Arctic Ocean

Europe

Asia

Africa

Pacific
Ocean

Indian
Ocean

Australia

Atlantic
Ocean

Antarctica

Whoosh! Oceans border Asia on three sides.

Asia's fourth side ends at the low Ural Mountains. These mountains lie between Asia and the continent of Europe.

Asia's 49 **countries** are grouped into six **regions.** They are North Asia, Central Asia, Southwest Asia, South Asia, Southeast Asia, and East Asia.

Brrr! Thick snow and ice cover North Asia most of the year. North Asia is also called Siberia.

The cold weather doesn't bother these reindeer in Siberia.

Deserts, mountains, and **plateaus,** or flat areas, make up Central Asia.

Many of the people of Central Asia
raise animals, such as sheep or goats.

Whew! Deserts also stretch across
much of Southwest Asia.

The Dead Sea is part of this region. The sea is the lowest place on Earth. People float easily in the sea's salty water.

Many mountain **chains** cut through South Asia. The Himalaya Mountains are the tallest.

Do you remember the tallest mountain?
It is called Mount Everest and is part of
the Himalaya chain.

Lots of rain falls on the lands and **islands** that make up Southeast Asia.

Farmers raise huge crops of rice in the region's rich, wet soil.

Large cities are found throughout East Asia. This is Tokyo, Japan.

China is the largest country in East
Asia. It has the most people of any
country in the world. This is the city of
Shanghai, China.

More than three billion people live in all the parts of Asia. They belong to hundreds of **ethnic groups.**

An ethnic group may share the same language and the same religion.

The number of people in South Asia is growing fast. This area may soon have more people than East Asia.

North Asia has the fewest people of any part of Asia. But it has the most land.

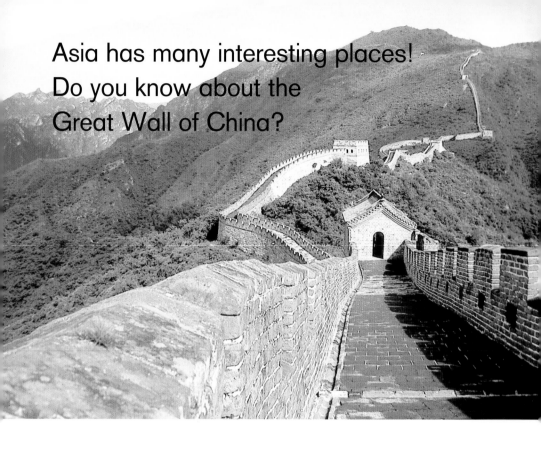

Asia has many interesting places!
Do you know about the
Great Wall of China?

It stretches for thousands of miles
in East Asia.

There's always something new to learn about Asia!

Cool Facts about Asia

- Asia covers more than 16 million square miles (44 million square kilometers).

- The large islands of Asia include Borneo, Hainan, Honshu, Luzon, Taiwan, and Sakhalin.

- The main rivers of Asia include the Amur River, the Ganges River, the Huang River, the Mekong River, the Ob River, and the Yangtze River.

- The animals of Asia include arctic foxes, Asian elephants, camels, giant pandas, tigers, and yaks.

- Plants living in Asia include date palm trees, mulberry trees, nutmeg trees, and olive trees.

- The large cities of Asia include Bangkok, Beijing, Calcutta, Hanoi, Jerusalem, Manila, Mumbai, Shanghai, Tashkent, and Tokyo.

Map of Asia

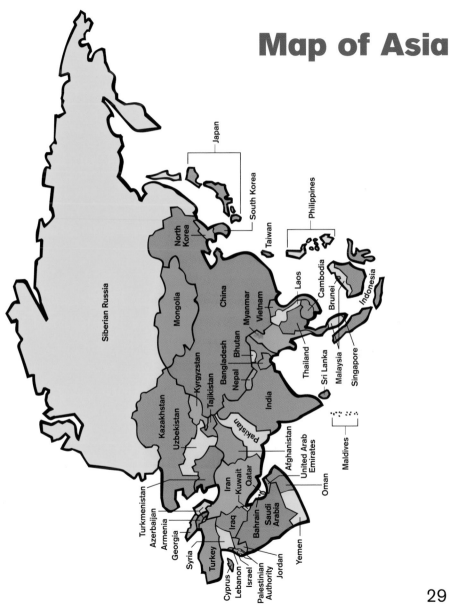

Glossary

chains: series of linked things. A mountain chain usually makes a long, thick line on a map.

continent: one of seven big pieces of land on Earth

countries: places where people live and share the same laws

ethnic groups: groups of people who have many things in common. They might speak the same language or follow the same religion.

islands: small pieces of land surrounded by water

plateaus: areas of high, flat land

regions: small parts of a larger piece of land

Further Reading and Website

Foster, Leila Merrell. *Asia.* Crystal Lake, IL: Heinemann Library, 2001.

Fowler, Allan. *Asia.* Danbury, CT: Children's Press, 2002.

Haskins, Jim. *Count Your Way through the Arab World.* Minneapolis: Carolrhoda Books, Inc., 1987.

Haskins, Jim. *Count Your Way through Israel.* Minneapolis: Carolrhoda Books, Inc., 1990.

Haskins, Jim. *Count Your Way through Korea.* Minneapolis: Carolrhoda Books, Inc., 1989.

Nelson, Robin. *Where Is My Continent?* Minneapolis: Lerner Publications Company, 2002.

Riehecky, Janet. *China.* Minneapolis: Carolrhoda Books, Inc., 1999.

Sayre, April Pulley. *Greetings, Asia!* Brookfield, CT: Millbrook Press, 2003.

Streissguth, Tom. *India.* Minneapolis: Carolrhoda Books, Inc., 1999.

Streissguth, Tom. *Japan.* Minneapolis: Carolrhoda Books, Inc., 1997.

Enchanted Learning

http://enchantedlearning.com/geography/asia

The geography section of this website has links to every continent.

Index